MIDDLE SCHOOL CHRONICLES

BY KEVIN

ISBN: 1490416331
ISBN 13: 9781490416335

Library of Congress Control Number: 2013913178
CreateSpace Independent Publishing Platform
North Charleston, South Carolina

TABLE OF CONTENTS

MY MIDDLE SCHOOL

THINGS YOU
WON'T BELIEVE

KEVIN

ONE LAST CHAPTER

DEDICATED TO MRS. FOBBS

This is a book about real things that happened in my middle school. The school is fictional, but the events are true. Some of them may make parents nervous, but maybe it will help them understand the world of a middle-school kid. The people mentioned are fictional, but they are based on real persons. Maybe you will recognize a teacher or student in the book, but that's because we humans are a lot alike and still very different. Finally, the book is about coming of age, growing up. "I hope kids will like to read this book. Parents should too."

KEVIN

MY
MIDDLE
SCHOOL

WELCOME TO BIRCH MEADOW

Hi, my name is Kevin. I am just finishing the sixth grade at Birch Meadow Middle School. I don't know why they call it Birch Meadow, since there are no birches anywhere around here and no meadow, either. There is lots of blacktop and a few playing fields. The blacktop is where the teachers park their cars and sneak out for a smoke. The playing fields are really busy when we go out for PE, or after school when sports start up.

The sixth grade is divided into three "teams," even though we don't actually compete or anything like that. The teams are named for fish. Honest to God, who ever thought this kind of stuff up? The teams are the Tunas, Whales, and Marlins. I am a Tuna, if you can believe it.

IT'S HARD TO DRAW YOURSELF. MAYBE I OVERDID MY BRACES.
I WANTED TO SHOW OFF MY FAVORITE T-SHIRT.

KEVIN

No one knows why anyone is on one team or another. We Tunas have just as many smart kids as the Whales or Marlins do. Frankly, I think the whole damned thing is fishy. My mom can almost make me barf with her teasing about it. "Here comes my favorite Tuna," she says. Cripes, I don't even like tuna fish.

I guess lots of people all over the world have been to middle school, but it's new for me. I never knew there would be so many things I would learn. I am not talking about language arts and math and stuff like that, but things that make being in middle school fun, sometimes silly, and even scary. The year has been a blast, except for getting in trouble, and that wasn't too much.

Let me tell you some things I have learned this last year, since I will soon be in the seventh grade. In fact, we are supposed to have a "fly up" day, which, by the way, makes no sense since we are not flying anywhere I know of. We are all supposed to go to the auditorium, where

HERE'S SIDNEY! HE'S A REAL DORK, BUT HE'S OUR DORK!

our principal, Sidney, will tell us about the "next steps on the ladder of knowledge." Honest to God, that's what he calls it.

While we are on the subject, let me tell you about Sidney. He thinks he is inspiring. What parent names a kid Sidney, for cripes' sake, especially one who will become principal of a middle school? Think about it. When you hear the name Sidney, you just think of a dork. Sidney lives up to his name. We all pick on him, but he doesn't know it. Sidney doesn't have a clue about the stuff that makes middle school a blast.

Sidney is tall. His suits don't fit too well and you can always see his socks. He has a really bald head that shines and even reflects light. He likes to stand in the front hall with his legs sort of apart, like a general bossing his troops around. He does some weird things like slapping his hands together over and over saying, "That's it, now, move along, move along." We speed up when we pass by him, but we slow down after and he doesn't know it. One kid in our class always gives Sidney the finger, but he hides it behind his back. Like I said, Sidney hasn't got a clue.

We wonder about Mrs. Sidney. Why did she marry a dork? Maybe he was different when she met him. Who knows, but she shouldn't let him out of the house in a suit that's too small for him.

Sidney came on the P.A. this morning with "Hello, boys and girls, and how are you today?" He loves the P.A. and the "boys and girls" thing. He begins each assembly with "OK, boys and girls, now settle down."

The older kids call Sidney a tool, which I guess is another name for weird. My dad says it is like being a "piece of work." Like I said, Sidney really likes the P.A., and he got himself into real trouble the other day. He got the entire school into lockdown. The teachers have been told that if Sidney comes on the P.A. with the code word

"Bruce," they are to lock their doors and pull the shades down over the windows into the hallway. We are all to be quiet in case a terrorist has invaded Birch Meadow. The other day Sidney piped up on the P.A. and said, "Would Mr. Bruce please come to the office" Bam. Thwack. Swish. Our room was instantly ready for the invasion. We all had to be quiet so whoever was storming the building would think we were not there and the door had just locked itself.

It turned out Sidney was calling for a substitute teacher named Mr. Bruce to come to the office. Sidney came back on the P.A. and said it was not a real alarm; he was just calling the substitute. We Tunas were in class with Mrs. Fobbs, our language arts teacher. She said she was not going to unlock the door since Sidney might be being held at gunpoint by whoever had gotten into Birch Meadow to do us all harm. She wouldn't open up until Frazier, the school janitor, came to the door and unlocked it. Even

THIS IS JEFF, MY BEST FRIEND. HE'S REALLY
ATHLETIC, BUT HE DOESN'T LOOK IT.

then, she had to be certain Frazier was not just reassuring her and we were out of danger.

My best friend is Jeff. He is one grade ahead of me. We were together in kindergarten, but I stayed in a "readiness" class back then. Readiness meant I needed more time to mature, I guess. The whole idea was stupid. Jeff went ahead, but we are still friends. Jeff is athletic and taller than I am. His grades are not as good as mine. I am usually on the honor roll but don't have to work too hard to get there. Maybe the readiness thing helped after all. Jeff has red hair, which he hates. The hair kind of matches his personality, if you know what I mean. He is always ready for a new adventure. More about that later.

Jeff and I both have braces. Jeff is also fitted with a thing in the roof of his mouth, and he complains about it. It makes him sound funny. "S" comes out as "th." "Thith thing maketh me talk thort of funny," he says. I agree. My braces are going to be on for two more years. By high school I will be done with them. They are not supposed to hurt, but they do, especially when they get tightened. Dr. Peigel, my orthodontist, always looks bored, but I think he gets a charge out of tightening braces. Maybe he had a bad childhood, and this is his revenge.

In my grade I have another best friend, Carl. He is a lot like me, and we do some stuff together. He likes video games, maybe more than I do. Too much of them can be boring, I think. I like to skateboard and longboard, and stuff like that. Carl does too. Jeff comes with us sometimes when he isn't busy with his teams. Carl is shorter than I am, a little on the heavier side, and gets called gay a lot, which he isn't. All Carl would have to do is sit on the kids who tease him. He would crush them on the spot.

All of us talk about Birch Meadow, Sidney, and lots of other things. Some things that have happened at our school are just weird. Others are funny. Most of them are ridiculous, but they are all true, and together they will give you an idea of what Middle School is like. Your parents may wish you had not read about it, since Middle School probably didn't even exist when they were our age. I'll show you what I mean. At this very minute Sidney has a real mystery on his hands. He thinks he is kind of like a detective, a Sherlock type. The mystery is about a kid no one would ever suspect. His name is Claude Flathers, which rhymes with blathers. Everyone thinks Claude is a nerd, but he will fool you. He is more strange than nerdy. Claude thinks it's cool to piss in lots of places outside the boys' room if you know what I mean. He strikes while Sidney isn't looking. Claude has left his calling card behind the lobby outside the auditorium, right near Sidney's office. It's driving our beloved principal crazy. Sidney is stalking Claude, kind of sneaking around, hoping to catch him in the act.

Frazier, the janitor, has to clean up the mess before parents' night so the place won't smell like an MTA station. I don't think Sidney is any match for Claude, who can piss quicker than anyone you ever saw and then walk on down the hall like an altar boy. We have taken to calling him the "power pisser," and no one has told Sidney anything, at least not yet.

Don't let me give you the wrong idea. There is a lot more to Birch Meadow than our principal.

Aside from Sidney, there are things that I wonder about, like who ever thought of the name "middle school"? What are we in the middle of? I'm just teasing; I know we are supposed to be in the middle of our development, which means, I think, the puberty thing or whatever. Grownups make a big deal out of puberty. Actually it doesn't mean much to me yet, but I have noticed I smell more like gym socks than I used to. Also, things are getting a little hairy, if you know what I mean.

The girls have been growing faster than us boys for a while. They are more interested in us than we are in them, but we pretend otherwise. No one wants to be called gay, so we act like we want to do stuff with them.

Oh yeah, while I'm at it, let me tell you about "gay." The word isn't what it used to be. It certainly doesn't mean happy. Sometimes it means a kind of unusual thing: "That's gay, man." "What a gay thing to do." And it can be a way of bullying someone: "You're gay." Most of the time is has nothing to do with really being gay, liking someone of your own sex, if you know what I mean. It just means not the usual thing and all that. It's a word we call each other, but we don't mean it literally.

Since Birch Meadow is a school, maybe I need to tell you about some of the grownups, teachers and others, that make the place a school. But before that I want to explain how Jeff and I got in trouble. I call this a "dumb day."

It all started when Jeff said something. I thought he was joking, but he wasn't. He had already shown me a few things about Birch Meadow when the year started—remember, he's in seventh grade, so he had a year of middle-school experience under his belt by the time I started at Birch Meadow. Jeff is an adventurous guy, the kind of kid who will go on a roof and jump off. He would do things like the people in those *Jackass* movies.

It was more than halfway through the school year. We were walking down the hall when he said, "Hey, Kev, why don't we skip school?"

I laughed, but he was serious.

When Jeff kept talking about it, I began to see he really wanted to do it. The winter was just about over, and the days were not as cold as they had been. Besides all that, I didn't want to be a wuss and a chicken, and Jeff was certain he had the whole thing worked out. Still, I told him I didn't think we should be doing this, that it was kind of advanced, something kids usually wait to do in high school.

Anyway, the day was a Monday. It was sunny, a great day to take some time off. Jeff said we could go to his house and hang out playing video games, getting on the computer, watching movies on TV, and all that. It would be a blast.

I was nervous about it but thought, "Why not? We all have to grow up sometime, and I was almost through with the sixth grade.

After we got off the school bus that morning, we walked around behind the school and took a kind of different path to Jeff's house. It was a few blocks away, and we passed a store where we picked up some colas and chips to take to his house for our day off.

What could go wrong? The whole thing was planned out. The whole thing was beginning to be fun.

After we got to Jeff's house, he checked to make sure no one had come home unexpectedly. His mom was at work.

Then the craziest thing happened, something you could never imagine in a million years. Jeff tripped over a stool in his living room and fell face down on his carpet. It was a pretty good thump, and his face really smacked the carpet. He was kind of kissing the floor. The trouble was Jeff couldn't get up.

He wasn't paralyzed or anything awful like that. No, his braces had tangled in the fibers of the carpet. I don't mean that his braces just brushed the rug. They were really, seriously tangled in it.

At first I couldn't understand what the problem was. Jeff made some sound like "Myf maces ur innerug." Then he said, "Icchant gitup." Finally I figured out what he was telling me. I tried to get him out of his tangle, but it was no use. He started to bleed all over his mom's rug, and I think he said some swear words, at least I think he did.. It was hard to understand him.

I started to worry—no, panic. This was karma. I had worried we would be found out, but not this. I couldn't leave him here to be discovered when his mom came home from work. Besides, he could bleed to death on the carpet.

I decided to call for help. Nine-one-one was a possibility, but how do you explain what two middle-school guys are doing in a house with no adults, and one of them is bleeding on the carpet? Besides, 911 would probably send an ambulance and all the neighbors would come out to gawk and all that. I could call our parents, but they need time to think about what happened before they ground you for the rest of your natural life.

So I called the school. The receptionist is Miss Emma. When she answered "Birch Meadow School," it all came out. I said we were at someone's house and "we have a situation here." I told her I was standing by my friend whose braces were tangled in the carpet. Miss Emma laughed and hung up. The whole thing was too ridiculous for her to believe.

So I called the school back. This time Miss Emma got the story, more or less, and said she would call Jeff's mom.

Sure enough, Jeff's mom came home. It turned out Sidney had called her about the "situation." She was not happy, not at all. She was not as mad over our skipping school as she was about the orthodontics cost and the blood staining her new carpet. She was also mad about having to leave work and having to explain the "stupidity," as she described it, of her son getting "tied up on the living room rug."

We both had to go back to school and have a session with Sidney. He gave us both five detentions.

My parents were not just unhappy. They were worried I had started down a path to "juvenile delinquency," as my dad put it. He went on and on but finally stopped when he grounded me for a month.

The story finally got out at school. Jeff took the worst, with kids laughing and calling him "rug face" and stuff like that.

I decided it is best to think before you do something stupid. And if I ever cut school again, I will make sure my friend has hardwood floors.

In addition to all this, I had to explain to my girl-friend, Melissa, what had happened. She said she was "disappointed." By the way, I know you haven't heard about Melissa, but I will explain all that later.

TEACHERS AND CLASSES

We notice things about our teachers. The truth is the teachers think they are watching us, but we are really figuring them out. Some of the teachers in our school like us. You can tell who they are. They want us to do OK. Others really don't like kids our age. No one knows why they take and keep the job, but we have our ways of helping them wish they had worked someplace else.

The first thing you notice about teachers are the little things. Señorita Carmina teaches Spanish. She is one of the nice teachers, even if she does have stains under her armpits. At lunch we have discussed whether she has her clothes cleaned and why she hasn't noticed she could use a few new things to wear. Teaching Spanish must make you sweat.

THIS IS OUR SOCIAL STUDIES TEACHER. HIS MOUTH IS OPEN, WHICH IT USUALLY IS. YOU CAN ALMOST HEAR HIM SAYING, "UH–HUH, SO YES THEN..."

Miss Crawford, the math teacher for some in our grade, has eyebrows that have grown together. We can't figure out if she knows she has them and why she hasn't had them waxed or whatever you do when you have too much eyebrow. It makes her look a little like an earlier model of a human—probably good for a math teacher.

You notice things about how someone speaks. Our social studies teacher puts an "uh-huh yes then" in all his classroom lectures. For instance, if he were talking about Abraham Lincoln, he would say, "So, class, Lincoln left Illinois by train for the trip to Washington. Uh-huh yes then. His trip was made difficult by a threat on his life. Uh-huh so yes then." We have taken to imitating him when we tell a good joke: "Have you heard the one about...uh-huh yes then."

There are other things that get our attention, such as with Mr. Kraus, the technology teacher. That, by the way, is a fancy name for someone who teaches computers.

Mr. Kraus has hair growing out of his nose. His nostrils sort of explode into this bushy stuff that looks like an untrimmed hedge. What's worse is how he bends over your shoulder to check what you are doing on the computer. The hedge looks like it might actually fall out on you. It is disgusting except you want to laugh. He wouldn't know what you were laughing about so that would not be good.

Kraus also wears dirty pants. I mean the pant pockets are stained like his hands have left tracks. He doesn't smell bad or anything like that. It just looks like someone hasn't been watching out for him. He is not married, and all of us are wondering if he is gay.

Language arts teachers are weird. Ours is named Mrs. Fobbs. She wears glasses that slip down on her nose, and lots of perfume. When she passes by your desk, you want to pass out from the smell. She has us read these dumb books that no one likes. Then we have to write what we think of them. I wrote, "This book sucks," but I didn't

MRS. FOBBS IS PROBABLY NOT THIS HOMELY. MY DRAWING
OF HER IS MORE ABOUT HOW I FEEL THAN HOW SHE LOOKS.

really plan on turning it in to her. Somehow it got mixed up with other papers in my backpack and she saw it. She almost cried, or looked like she was going to. She went on about how much teaching mattered to her and how hard she worked to get us to understand the "deeper things of life," as she put it.

What really gets to me is LA teachers wanting us to interpret things. With the book that I said sucked, she had asked us to think about the meaning of the cloud in one chapter. I said it was just a cloud. She kind of smirked like I didn't get it. Then, after everyone had told her one thing or another they thought she wanted to hear, she said the cloud was a symbol for the passing of life, a kind of spiritual thing. She kind of got emotional when she was explaining it.

We all looked like we knew what she was talking about, but I don't have a clue. To me it is just a damned cloud. I sure hope my life doesn't pass like that! Maybe that's her problem—you know, life passing like a cloud and all that. Maybe she needs help.

I do not like language arts. The language we speak is OK. I can write, and I love to read, especially the Harry Potter books. What I hate is when you write something the teacher wants a "draft." I thought that was what my dad likes in beer. What the teacher wants is a "first draft." Then you turn it in and she hands it back with red marks all over it. My draft looked like it had bled to death, for cripes' sake. Then you have to do it over and maybe again. By that time I am bored with the whole thing, which I wasn't too happy about to start with.

Don't get me wrong. There's stuff that the teachers tell us that I really like. Take space, for instance, and the planets and the universe. That makes me understand where we came from. I want to know why we are here, and what was here before all this was. I don't know if other kids think about this stuff like I do, but it is interesting.

When I brought space up at lunch, the group at the table stopped talking. They sort of thought I was strange, or at least that's what I felt. But one of the guys was interested. We got to talking about how hot it must be on Venus and how long it would take to get to the nearest star and all that. The truth is not everyone will like the same things you do, but there is always someone who does.

Our science teacher is named Mr. Finkelstein. He really gets into the universe and the planets. He likes for us to get into it too. I think I will get a good grade in science, and this should make my parents happy. It seems like teachers want you to like the same things they do. I guess I am lucky. It is good to wonder and be curious and to have teachers who feel the same way like Mr. Finkelstein.

I'm sorry, but I am not done talking about LA or Mrs. Fobbs. Language arts brings out some nutty stuff in adults. Teachers can get worked up over the strangest things. Mrs. Fobbs was reading *Gunga Din* by this English writer. It was about this Indian kid who was helping the British troops or something like that. The kid was getting ragged on. In this day and age the ones making him do things would be arrested for child abuse. Well, she was reading this poem and getting emotional about the kid. We all thought she was going to cry. Then, out of the blue, she started laughing. God knows why. We thought she might be having a breakdown if you know what I mean. It turns out she does this every year. It is kind of like an act, her way of making you remember the poem. I have forgotten the poem, but I will remember her breakdown. Poems just get to some people, I guess. The eighth-graders say she did the same thing when they were in her class, and they wondered if she were going to have to be taken away.

Mrs. Fobbs has been on my case. She says I use phrases that don't have any purpose. She is really upset that I say "if you know what I mean" too much. I have sometimes written this in my assignments. It beats me why this is so bad. "If you know what I mean" says exactly what I mean. So there. But I guess when Mrs. Fobbs is around I will have to say it some other way. Maybe I could say, "Are you following me?," but she probably wouldn't like that either. That's just how LA teachers are, if you know what I mean. She has also fussed about my saying "and all that" too much. She thinks I should say clearly what "all that" is. How can I? It's just "all that."

Why we can't talk more about Harry Potter annoys me. Ms. Fobbs said she was going to focus on "more serious literature." If the stuff she came up with is "serious," then count me out. I would rather talk about Harry Potter, why he couldn't make it with Hermione and why Malfoy was such an idiot and all that.

Speaking of Malfoy, every class has one. In language arts it is Clarence Smith. He sucks up to the teacher, and when she calls on one of us, he smirks because he always says what makes her happy. She doesn't get it. Clarence actually hates language arts as much as the rest of us do, but he knows the teacher will spaz out with joy when he butters her up. If our teacher were a biscuit, she would have enough butter on her to float in it.

This brings me to math. What is it about math teachers? Ours, Miss Crawford, has glasses, a long nose, and no smile. The last time she broke into a smile, the heavens opened. There's no danger of the heavens losing it over her. Miss Crawford—and I emphasize the "Miss" part—lives for factoring and finding "x." She could never find a man who would want to talk about equations and multiplication, fractions and that kind of thing. She would bore him to death like she does us when she goes on about something she has put on the Smart Board. She knows what she is talking about, but we have trouble getting it. Of course, Clarence is in my math class, and he tries his tricks with Miss Crawford. She frosts

I TOLD YOU SHE WAS HOT!

him. "Clearly Clarence does not know what he is talking about," she says. The whole class practically applauds.

There is one teacher I really like. She teaches art. I usually don't like art, since they give you dumb things like Popsicle sticks and expect you to make something out of them. To me they still look like a pile of Popsicle sticks. Last year in the fifth grade at my elementary school there was this nut case who kept on talking about "art in everyday life." We were supposed to draw our shoes. I had trouble finding much art in my shoes, but I gave it a try. She shook her head when I handed her my drawing. It never got on the bulletin board with the others.

This year is different, and the teacher, Miss Friedlander, is young and what the eighth-graders would call "hot." I think she is really pretty, kind of a work of art all by herself. One day she called me to her desk.

"Kevin," she said. God, I loved how she said my name.

"Yes, Miss Friedlander," I said. I hope I didn't show her how I felt. My face was kind of hot, maybe red.

She smiled and handed me a paper.

"I looked at your drawings, and you have real talent. This is a note for you to tell you how much I think of what you are doing. Keep it up."

Good God, she doesn't have to worry. I am beginning to know what "hot" means. I hope no one knows the fantasies I have about her. I would love sketching her in the... well, you know what I mean.

"Hot" brings me to another subject and teacher. For some reason, we have to take sex education as part of health class. Health, in the sixth grade, should be called "sex, drugs, and rock and roll." The teacher, Ms. Trilling, is serious, even kind of stone-faced. I don't think she likes teaching about the sex part, but she does OK with nutrition and gives lots of warnings about drugs.

For the drug part, a police officer came in with a kind of board showing all the kinds of drugs people use. He said these were real drugs and told us about each one. They had some pictures of people with "before" and "after" on them. These were people who took stuff they were not supposed to. One was a woman who looked kind of hot in her first picture. In the second picture she had fewer teeth and really bad skin. The officer said it was taken after she had used something called "crystal."

Then there was a sex part of the class. We wondered how Ms. Trilling would talk about sex.

At lunch we wondered if she had ever had sex, but since she has three kids she talks about, we guessed she had. We also kind of wondered about Mr. Trilling and if she was always as stone-faced with him. Maybe living with him and having three kids was why she is stone-faced. We didn't know, even though we had lots of ideas.

The boys are separated from the girls for "the films," as Ms. Trilling calls them. The films are not like a porn thing. One is a close-up of a woman giving birth to a child. When I say close, that's what I mean. The camera zooms right in, and you can see the baby being pushed out. Really, I would rather watch almost any film than this, but Ms. Trilling calls it "the process." I guess I am happy I was "processed," but I'm really glad I can't remember it. If you make any wisecracks during the film, you get sent straight to guidance for a talk with Mr. Strong. That could be about as bad as childbirth.

The guys agree we are happy to never have this happen to us. It looks like it would hurt a lot, and the woman did not look like she was having fun. When the baby finally popped out, they kind of wiped it off and handed it to the woman. She was definitely tired and beat but she smiled when she held the baby. I don't know if it was a boy or a girl since the whole thing was so disgusting I didn't watch. The whole thing makes me happy to be a dude and also thankful to have a mom. I am going to tell her I really am happy to be her kid, but I will not go into why.

The second film about the "process" was really kind of fun. It was a cartoon about how babies get made. It showed a stick man and woman having sex. The sound effects were terrific. The bed squeaked. The best part was the cartoon sperm who kind of zoomed around as if it were powered by a rocket or something. We all got the point, and there were some laughs. It was much better than the childbirth film.

Health education, which, as I said, is mostly about drugs and sex, comes just before lunch. It took a while for my appetite to come back, but I have recovered enough to eat two helpings of chicken fingers and two chocolate milks.

By the way, I'd better enjoy the chocolate milks while I can. They say they will be serving plain milk from now on. The chocolate is supposed to be bad for you.

There is one class that is real food for thought: home economics. The name is confusing since all we do is pop popcorn and make brownies. The best thing is eating the stuff we make. Our teacher is Mrs. Phlak—definitely a strange name, worse than Sidney. Some kids call her Mrs. Flake but only behind her back. She starts everything she says with "now, class": "Now, class, today we are going to make some brownies." She must have eaten a lot of her own cooking because she is larger than a small school bus. She is cheerful, though, and seems to like seeing us make things and enjoy them. That's more than I can say for your average language arts teacher.

Miss Flora is our music teacher. She really loves what she does but can get a little angry when we don't show respect for "the arts." She told us her name means "flower." She is a really big flower, if you know what I mean. In fact, Miss Flora is more like a tree, a large bush, or a big vase with a whole bouquet.

THIS IS MISS FLORA AFTER SHE HIT THE
FLOOR. YOU CAN ALMOST SEE HER MOUTH
SINGING "IN THE BEAUTY OF THE LILIES..."

She likes to sing and tries to teach us to do songs too. "From the diaphragm" is one of her favorite things to say. She also wants us to say words in a funny way when we sing. She kind of purses up her mouth and turns it into a small cave when she hits a note. She wants us to sing "The Battle Hymn of the Republic" for the end-of-year assembly when parents will be there. She is trying to get us to sing "in the beauty of the lilies" as "een the beauutyyy off the lilliees." "You must enunciate," she says. When we don't do it right, she sinks into her chair behind the teacher's desk in the music room. She seems sad and disappointed.

She sank all of her many pounds onto her chair a week ago. Her legs are like those on a piano, and she let go when she sat down. The chair couldn't take it. It broke into all kinds of pieces, and Miss Flora wound up in a big heap on the floor. "Oh shit," she said with great enunciation.

Some of us tried not to, but the class broke up in lots of laughs. A couple of us tried to help her up. She did most of the getting up herself. It's a good thing, since we could have been injured ourselves.

Miss Flora was out for a week. Word got around that Sidney heard about the swearing when the chair broke. He was sympathetic to Miss Flora and the chair, but he told her that swearing in front of sixth-graders was unprofessional. She has returned, and the school looks like it has given her a new and better chair. It's a good thing, and we will be ready for "The Battle Hymn of the Republic."

DANGER— GUIDANCE OFFICE

The guidance office is a place you want to stay out of. You will be guided, alright—into trouble. The door has big letters on it that say "Guidance." For cripes' sake, why advertise what is going on? It's like the sign is saying you don't know where you are going but can find out here.

Mr. Strong, the guidance counselor, has the place decorated with weird pictures. One is of an elephant with its trunk in the air like it is sniffing for peanuts or something. The other is of a street scene. Some people are sort of staring at each other and drinking alcohol, I think. They look like they have just had a counseling session with Mr. Strong. He has another sign on his door. "In

Session," it says. When you go in, he turns the sign over and everyone knows what is going on.

The worst thing is Strong's big mouth. Anything you say will be used against you to your parents or in the faculty room. "Well, you know," Strong will say, "with his family and what has been going on...." You can bet Strong is the tunnel for information that goes everywhere.

When you go for a session, one-word answers are best. "How are you doing?" is answered by "fine." If you want him to write nice things about you and your family, you answer the question "Are you having any problems?" with "nope" or "no, sir."

You can tell Strong takes himself really seriously. He answers the phone with "Strong here," as if he were lifting weights and being interrupted by someone.

I don't believe I mentioned the curtains on the windows. They aren't like the other curtains at our school. They look more like tank tops sewn together. God, I hope they aren't Strong's tank tops, and if they are, let's hope he washed them first!

Strong tries to see all of us at one time or another, but his real job is for the serious cases, kids who have gotten themselves noticed for stuff. Sidney sends just about all the tough cases to Strong for a mental tune-up. Strong tries to get into your mind. That is just weird, something you don't want to let him do. When parents come in, it is a really big deal. They all march down the hall like some kind of execution is about to happen, and you definitely don't want to be the main guest.

Like I said, nothing good ever comes from being sent to guidance. Mr. Strong is strange, no doubt about it. He smiles at you and says uh-huh and stuff like that. He comes to school dressed strange too, like he wears two different colored socks. For lunch he eats cucumbers with a kind of creamy stuff on them. The stuff drips down his chin, and he wipes it off with a red handkerchief. Even though his name is Mr. Strong, he isn't. He couldn't bench-press a dollar bill without losing his wind.

I was called down once and asked how I was "settling in" and if I was enjoying my "middle-school experience." I told him I was very excited, which was a lie, but I knew if I told him only a nerd likes being in school, he would think I needed counseling. Then I would probably be scheduled on his lunch hour and have to watch him eat those queer cucumbers.

One kid got sent because he didn't know when to keep his mouth shut. This was Jim Weaks, kind of one of my friends, even though he is two grades ahead of mine. In Mrs. Trilling's eighth grade health class he spoke up when he should have kept quiet. The boys were being talked to away from the girls so as not to embarrass either group. The teacher, one of the guys who teach science, brought in a banana and a condom. He put the condom on the banana to show how it was done. Personally, I can't believe anyone would be stupid enough not to know how a con-dom is supposed to be used, but the teacher thought it was important to demonstrate. Weaks held up his hand and the teacher said, "Yes, Mr. Weaks?" Weaks said, "Isn't that kind of a waste of a good banana?" The science teach-er got angry. He was, he said, trying to make a point. He thought Weaks was just being funny. He said Weaks was "disrespectful." I couldn't see what the big deal was.

But Weaks was sent to Mr. Strong's office for a tune-up. Now think about it: here were Weaks and Strong, dis-cussing sex education and a banana.

Rumor has it they are not using bananas any more. Naturally, the talk at lunch centered on what other fruits or vegetables would be good. Some kids thought maybe a gherkin would be it. I wanted a butternut squash. That's the kind of thing we talk about at lunch, definitely not with Mr. Strong.

I have my own story about trouble and Strong.

There was this poking thing that landed me in Strong's office. One day Ernie Linback, a dweeb and a nerd, decided to poke me for some reason. I guess it was funny to him. After about five pokes, I asked him to please stop. He thought it was just friendly, but the pokes kind of hurt. Then, he started again, even after I told him to stop. So I told him if he didn't stop I was going to punch him in the nose, no kidding. Ernie didn't think I meant it, so he kept poking.

I wheeled around and landed a pretty good one right up on his nose. He started to bleed and cry at the same time. The teacher came over and said, "Kevin, what did you do?" She didn't ask what Ernie had done. She said I would have to go see Sidney, but when I went to his office, he wasn't in. Miss Emma said I should go straight to guidance, where Mr. Strong would handle the whole matter. When we got to Strong's office, he turned over the "In Session" sign. He didn't seem to want to hear my side of the story. He said the school had a zero-tolerance policy about violence, and he was really worried about where I was heading.

According to Strong, I had a bad future, filled with Ernies and pokes and violence and all that. I had made someone's nose bleed. He asked if I was proud of myself. I said no, but I was, kinda. At least Ernie had stopped poking.

But you would not believe what happened next. Strong sent for the physical therapist. She does things with rubber balls, brushes, and other weird stuff. She nodded as Strong told her about the horrible thing I had done. Then I had to sit and squeeze this stupid ball for almost forty minutes. She went on about how I needed "strategies" for my violent tendencies.

My folks arrived. Strong had called them. I was actually glad to see them and be able to get away from Strong and that damned therapist and her stupid ball. The good

ACTUALLY, MELISSA'S PRETTIER THAN THIS. THIS IS KIND OF HOW SHE LOOKED AFTER OUR KISS. I'M NOT SURE IF SHE WAS DISAPPOINTED.

news is I got suspended for a day to think about what I had done. At least it was a day off from school. Ernie didn't get a thing except sympathy for getting a bloody nose from the most violent kid in the sixth grade.

My visits with Strong were really silly. The lady with the ball was even sillier. But I guess the whole thing turned out alright.

Strong has one other topic that he thinks is important: he is really big on talking about puberty. I wish he would stop. I know it is happening. We all do. I don't need to hear it from him. I have trouble even imagining Strong going through puberty.

Most anything we do gets a knowing look from an adult and blamed on puberty, on what Strong calls "awakening feelings." I am not sure why puberty gets so much attention. As far as I can tell, the eighth-graders are loud, swear a lot, and smell worse than we do. That is not much to say about some dumb change everyone carries on about.

There is one other thing that happens but I am not going to go there. Eighth-graders "go out" more than we do. In sixth grade, when we say "going out," we aren't really going anywhere, much less doing anything. But the eighth-graders are. Sidney talks about it on the P.A. The eighth-graders do stuff like practicing mouth-to-mouth rescue in the back hall. They also do grinding without any music.

Other than kissing Melissa, which was more her idea, I can't say that what the eighth-graders are doing looks like huge fun. That will probably change, but for now, puberty is just beginning, I guess. Some hair is turning up, and my ma has given me the deodorant speech. I use it because it actually smells kind of good in a manly kind of way.

My dad says this is the best time of my life. He gets kind of soft when he talks about it. Sometimes he has to tell me what it was like for him. It's kind of strange, but I like to hear his stuff. He came through it all alright, and I guess I will too, even though I am not sure what "it" is.

With all this stuff going on I have only one piece of advice: stay out of Strong's office unless you want to wind up talking about puberty and squeezing some damned ball.

IMPORTANT PEOPLE

Teachers are important, I guess, but they don't make Birch Meadow run. The really neat people are not teachers. Three other people don't get much attention, but they have a lot of stuff they do.

Frazier is my first important nonteacher person. He is the school janitor and he is old, maybe even fifty. He knows more about Birch Meadow than anyone. He is like Hagrid in Harry Potter except he doesn't have any magic animals or stuff like that. Frazier is kind of tall and moves in a rambling way. Then again, he can boogie down the hall pretty fast if he has to. He is a friend to all of us and sometimes keeps things we do from Sidney. Like Hagrid, Frazier is on our side.

The school nurse is OK, but she will only call your parents if you are sick. She will tell you to lie down on one of her couches or send you back to class if you have no temperature. Really, it is Frazier who takes care of us and cleans our barf in the hall when we are sick and can't make it to the bathroom. He never seems to mind; he brings his disinfectant sawdust and his trusty mop to clean up what to us is like a catastrophe. The nurse just takes your temperature or gives you an aspirin or says you will be alright. Frazier cares. For him it is personal, if you know what I mean.

There are some secrets Frazier keeps. The roof of the school is one of them. There is a staircase on one end of our building, and a window opens to a rooftop. The locks on the window aren't always reliable, and I think Frazier knows it. We found out about it from older kids. You can climb through the window and go out on the roof. No one really wants to go out there until winter. After the

FRAZIER ALWAYS HAS A SMILE ON HIS FACE, EVEN WHEN
HE'S GOING TO UNPLUG THE TOILETS IN THE BOYS' ROOM.

snow comes, it's fun to lie down on the flat roof and make snow angels or throw snowballs and fun stuff like that. It really isn't as dangerous as it sounds, since there is a border on the roof that comes up to our waists. I guess someone could be stupid enough to climb over that and jump down two stories, but no one ever has. Someone said the eighth-graders go out on the roof in the spring to make out. I guess it would be a good place for that since it is kind of private.

Some guys think it is fun to stop up the toilets in the boys' room. They make natural products, if you know what I mean, and then overdo it on the toilet paper and paper towels. If enough of all of the stuff is in the toilet, the things overflow and Frazier has his work cut out for him. We know what's happened when we see him trudging down the hall with his plunger in hand.

Sidney has spoken about this on the P.A. "Boys and girls. I have put a sign in the boys' room." Why he is telling this to both the boys and girls beats me, but that's Sidney for you. The next day a sign was in each stall: "If it's brown, flush it down." Sidney must be a poet. Well, the sign didn't work, because the towels used to wipe your hands are brown, too, so everyone put a few handfuls in the toilet and then flushed. Frazier was back on the job. Sidney was in a snit.

While we are on the subject of towels, there is something else guys like to do. Wet paper towels stick to things. When you wet the hand towels, it's fun to toss them at the ceiling and see if they stick. Sometimes it's fun to toss them at each other. We have fun, but Frazier is the one who has to clean the mess up.

Sidney decided we should do the cleanup since we made the mess. The funny thing is that parents complained and so did Frazier. The parents were upset about their kids being asked to clean a bathroom instead of getting an education. I don't know why cleaning up a boys' room isn't kind of educational, but the parents really made a fuss. Then Frazier said he was angry because we were taking work away from him, and he would file a grievance, whatever that means.

Anyway, Sidney gave in. Frazier cleans up, but we have tried to keep the flying paper and stop-ups down.

Frazier has a kind of office under the stairs toward the back of the school. The stuff he cleans with is in there, including brooms, mops, and all the other things he needs. He has a chair and a table where he keeps his things. There's a light so he can read and relax in between things that go on.

The main thing Frazier does for most of the year is keep us warm. Birch Meadow has a big boiler down in the basement. I don't remember our elementary school having a room like this. It must have, but I never saw it. The boiler is really kind of scary. It's big and it has a roaring fire making steam for the whole school. Frazier is the one who knows how to start the thing and what to do when it acts up or makes too much noise. This makes him really important and, if you think about it, is kind of magic.

What I like most about Frazier is his way of being happy. He never seems to complain much and really enjoys his job. This is better than some of the other people in the school who don't seem to like us much. Maybe Frazier is smarter than they are.

Jeff, Carl, and I are some of Frazier's best friends. He will sort of let us get away with some things like running in the halls, crawling out a window, and other dumb stuff we do. He also laughs at our jokes.

In his little office down under the stairs, Frazier has pictures. His son is in the Marines, and Frazier is really proud of him. He said he thought we might make good Marines. I don't know about that. I am really lousy at doing pushups.

Other than Frazier, there are two other nonteachers, the school nurse and Miss Emma. I don't know Miss Emma's last name any more than I know Sidney's. Miss Emma is the school secretary. She sits in the front office, and she is really the most important person in our school except for maybe Frazier. When I say she sits, it is true. She is really large in the caboose, if you get what I mean. She is the one we bring class reports of attendance to. She takes up late notes and gives you a pass. She routes parents and kids all over the school. "You need to see the nurse, dear." "Go to your homeroom now." "Detention is down the hall, three doors on the left."

Miss Emma is usually good-humored. Hour after hour she is the voice of Birch Meadow. "Birch Meadow School, Miss Emma speaking," she says when she answers the phone, but she kind of sings it like a bird or something. The main thing she has to do is take care of Sidney, who is really helpless. She gets him to assemblies, tells him when to make announcements, and says who he will be seeing next.

Miss Emma never married and has no children. We are her kids, and she seems to be one of the people who really does enjoy her job. When she gets old, over fifty, and has to leave here, she will be lost. Maybe a man will come along and marry her so she can travel the world and do something besides take care of Sidney and chirp "Birch Meadow" all day.

Miss Emma has one problem: she can be absent-minded, especially with the P.A. system, which she turns on and off for Sidney. Why he can't do it is a mystery, but Miss Emma faithfully takes care of it for him.

When she forgets to turn it off, it can be entertaining. Sidney has a habit of complaining about his digestion, and he does it out loud. Miss Emma sympathizes with him, and the discussion can get sort of graphic:

Sidney: "My Lord, but something I ate doesn't agree with me. Everything is growling and I am just not getting relief. Maybe it's the cafeteria food. It is OK for the kids, but those chicken fingers have really upset me."

Miss Emma: "Oh, I know what you mean. I have not been quite right in my digestion since those chicken fingers. I think the cafeteria gets them from a food service in Chicago."

The cafeteria workers get to hear the whole thing. Every kid in school does too. Nobody wants to think about Sidney's digestion, if you know what I mean. It kind of upsets everyone's stomach. But it is true that the chicken fingers are not that good. Besides, who ever heard of a chicken with fingers?

Other than Frazier and Miss Emma, I guess the school nurse is someone we all know, one way or another. I think she has a great job. Our nurse is Mrs. Priscilla Gladstone, R.N. I think R.N. stands for "real nurse" or something like that. She is like a queen over her room, or maybe it is more like rooms. She has something they call the "health suite," but it makes no sense because you only go there when you are sick or want to get out of class. If you haven't studied for a test, you can always try to go to the nurse, but Gladstone, or Mrs. G. as she likes to be called, will probably figure you out and send you right back to the teacher.

Mrs. Gladstone is more stone than glad. She is what my mom calls "stout." Dad says women like that are just fat, but Mom is right. I bet Mrs. G. could bench-press close to her own weight, which is one reason no one wants to fool around on her.

If she thinks you are sick, Mrs. G does one of three things. She gives you an aspirin, tells you to lie down, or calls your parents and sends you home. She has a few beds in the health suite, imitation leather with a kind of paper thing across the foot and head rest. It is no fun being there as far as I am concerned.

Gladstone is not full of fun. "Have you had a BM? Have you vomited? Have you had any diarrhea?" She is downright personal and kind of thinks of herself as a real doctor. When you see her, you usually want to get better or get away. Once a year she checks eyes and hearing. She really gets to play doctor then. She also likes checking backs to see if we are growing straight. I am not sure why we need this in school, but I guess there is a reason for it.

The girls say she asks them about their period. "Are you having your period, dear?" Guys don't have to worry about that, thank God. I definitely don't want one—a period, I mean.

There was this time I tried to fool Mrs. G. I didn't want to stay in English since Fobbs was getting really boring, going on about poetry and beauty and all that. So I said I had to go to the nurse. I rubbed my stomach and did a great job of faking a sick face, kind of groaning. When Mrs. G. saw me she said, "Oh my goodness, we have something to fix all that!" She got a bottle of chalklike stuff off the shelf and began shaking it. It looked gross and a lot like the stuff my mother puts down my throat when I am faking being sick so I can stay home from school. The stuff is terrible and it will make you gag. If you weren't sick before, you will be after a spoonful of that, if you know what I mean.

So I had an amazing recovery and told Mrs. G. that I had miraculously gotten better and would be able to go back to class after all. She looked disappointed since I think she enjoys giving kids that stuff.

Even poetry is better than that stuff.

GIRLS

I never thought about girls being different from guys. Don't get me wrong, I have been paying attention. But I mean really different. The girls I liked in elementary school liked the same things the guys did. They played ball and tag and all that. The others were more like our moms and did stuff like shopping at the mall, wearing dresses, and even putting on lipstick. One or two carried purses.

Things changed a lot this year. I am not sure I want to be really close to a girl in what they say is "that way." The girls have changed. They are taller and they have bigger chests, if you know what I mean. They walk differently than I think they used to. It seems to me they find ways to be close to us guys. Some of them are very interesting to look at.

I started getting calls from this girl. Her name is Clarice, which in itself is not normal. No one names a kid Clarice. She called up my house and asked my dad if she could talk to me. Of course my dad made a big deal of it, asked her name, and winked and made a stupid face. I didn't want to talk about it at all. It was not a call I wanted, and it was none of my dad's business. Buy my folks have always told me to be kind to everyone, so I was at least nice to Clarice.

She didn't seem to have anything to say in her call except she wanted to know what I thought of different girls. I told her they were all OK. Then she wanted to know how I felt about her. I told her I felt fine as long as she was doing her thing and I was doing mine. She wanted to meet and talk some more. I said I was very busy. Maybe girls are into talking a lot. I don't know, but it is not a guy thing.

The story got more complicated because she was kind of stalking me. She would turn up at lunch and once even sat at a guy table. That was just not cool and was very embarrassing for me. One day at lunch she said the dumbest thing. "I am the macaroni," she said, "and you are the cheese." How dumb is that? The guys really teased me. "Hey, Kevin. Are you the macaroni or the cheese?" Then she turned up near my locker and kind of leaned on the door until I told her she would have to move so I could close it.

Finally I had to ask one of my friends to help out. A girl I know and who is more like a guy than a girl talked to her and said I was not ready for a relationship with anyone of her sex and it would be best to leave me alone.

The whole word "relationship" is kind of stupid. I don't really know what the whole thing means. You have a relationship with your relatives, like your aunt and uncle. Why do you have a relationship with a girl you don't even know except at school? You can have a relationship with a car because it runs fast or has nice lines and great fenders. I am not ready for Clarice's fenders or her lines, either.

On the other hand, I turned out to have my own "relationship."

It sounds kind of funny to talk about it, but lots of us are "going out" with someone now. I am now going out with Melissa—I won't give you her last name for obvious reasons. Melissa has been told by her parents she is not allowed to date. They don't know about me because we really don't go anywhere. It just means we are a couple in our grade and no one else should come between us. All the guys except the nerds are going out with someone, since you definitely don't want to be known as gay.

Melissa is a lot like a guy. She likes football and climbing trees. I don't think she ever played with dolls. The best thing about her is she likes me! She is beautiful and has long blonde hair. She isn't like the stupid jokes about people with her hair color. She is probably the smartest girl in the class unless you count Cheryl, who is a female nerd of the first order, wears thick glasses, and is not likely to win a beauty contest.

Melissa and I have held hands, although Sidney has spoken about public displays of affection, or PDA for short. He will stop even hand-holding if he sees it in the hallway. Since Melissa is not allowed to date, our relationship has been kind of secret. By the way, I never knew holding hands could be as fun as it turns out to be. I guess I have not had much experience in hand-holding until Melissa.

One day she told me she loved me, and I didn't know exactly what to say, so I said, "Ditto," and that seemed to please her. Then Melissa decided we should kiss each other. She planned the time and place. I wasn't too clear about how to go about it since I had never kissed anyone except my aunts and parents. I practiced a few times using the bathroom mirror. I made sure the door was locked before I practiced my technique.

Melissa and I walked to the back hall of our school where we did kiss. It was OK but not all that great. She tasted like chewing gum, and she said she had treated herself to some spearmint earlier in the morning. I was a little worried about the braces since we both have them. If they had gotten tangled, we would have been in guidance for the rest of our lives.

Melissa was my first. I don't think I will ever forget her, even the peppermint taste of the first kiss. But great things have an end, and the worst has happened. Melissa called me the other night. She was almost whispering because she didn't want her parents to know she was talking to a boy. Cripes, what is their problem? She has an older brother so they must know something I don't.

Anyway, Melissa said she hated to be the one to tell me, but she thought we had better stop going out. She said we should move on with our lives and find other people. I didn't have the heart to tell her it was OK with me.

The whole going out thing is just something else to worry about. I mean, with skateboarding and other things you want to do, you have to worry about going out and finding time to visit in the back hall, keeping secrets, and all that. This relationship thing is complicated.

So I am moving on with my life and Melissa seems to be doing OK with hers. She is also walking a lot with the nerd's nerd, Grafton. Maybe she is helping him move on also. I am bothered by one thing, though. Did she break up because I was not a good kisser? I know I have to be better at kissing than Grafton.

There is a lot more about girls I want to learn. Melissa has started my imagination working. Mom says I should not be in a hurry. I think I will take her advice, except maybe for this girl Penny, who has just broken up with her boyfriend.

Penny is a girl I call Six Cents. This is a play on her name, Penny Nichol—get it? Penny and nickel, six cents.

Penny is fun, more like a guy, if you know what I mean. She likes hanging out with us and talking about sports and video games and all that. Penny is kind of big. She has grown a lot in the last year. Some of the guys tease her about her build, which is big around the chest and all. But they don't push her too far because she would deck them. They say she came to our town from the city, where she learned to be tough and not take anything from anybody.

Six Cents has been written up by a couple of teachers. She gives them what my folks call "back talk." Our math teacher, Miss Crawford, was on her case about something, and Six Cents said "whatever" better than any kid I ever knew. The teacher went ballistic. Six Cents just looked at her with that "go pound sand" kind of stare. Her grades are not great. I sure hope they move her on to the next grade because I would miss having her around.

I don't know why, but another kid I think is funny is Twilla. We call her Twilla Light, like the movies. Actually,

Twilla would be great in one of those movies because she is blonde and hot. She gets noticed but not just because of her body: she is the best cheater you ever saw. Twilla is not great in the smarts department, but she can cover herself with quiz answers. She writes things on her arm, even between her fingers. She never looks at anyone else's work or takes a quick read of a paper. It is all written on her body. She is a walking library of information written so carefully that no teacher has ever seen it. Her grades are good but her brain is empty, since all her info goes down the drain when she showers.

Maybe something will work out with Six Cents and me. She is adventurous, if you know what I mean.

Still, Twilla is interesting. The girl thing will be part of seventh grade. That will give me time to think about it over the summer.

THE LUNCH ROOM

You would think that with a name like Birch Meadow, the lunch room would be a beautiful place, maybe overlooking meadows and birches, with music and birds chirping and all that. It's not. It is an auditorium, gym, and lunch room all in the same space. The lights are all that shine in this place. The smells are a combination of gym socks and sloppy joes, the specialty of the house. The tables are like ones you see in prison movies, kind of like picnic tables but made of some kind of metal that can be hosed down after lunch.

Sidney calls this place a "cafetorium," which is a word you probably won't find in a dictionary. It is a combination of cafeteria and auditorium. Somehow "gym" isn't part of the word. There is a definite odor of sweat in the place, though. Maybe it could be a "sweatatorium." And then the bathrooms could be called "crapatoriums." Even Fobbs would have to admit, the English language is wonderful.

Now, what passes for food is not what your mom thinks it is. Lunches are almost three dollars. For this you get sloppy joes, which deserve their name, a half pint of milk, and some curled up green leaves they call a salad. The salad is swimming in something, mostly vinegar. We think the sloppies are made from that recycled beef they show on television documentaries. The whole thing is served by ladies my mom would describe as "going through the change," or, as my Aunt Maddie says, are visited by the "monthly curse," whatever that is. They can be moody— sometimes nice, and then cranky. "Hi there," they say on their better days, and on others, "Make up your mind. I haven't got all day."

The good thing about the lunch room is that it's one of the only places we can be social and talk. Lunch period is only twenty minutes long, but most of us eat pretty fast. We have to. Jeff has a different lunch period because he is in a grade ahead of me, so Carl and me and even Pomfert, or "Porn Fart," often eat at the same table. What table you eat at is important. We might be called the skateboard table. Some would call us skateboard punks, but we're not. We are good students, but we know it isn't cool to admit it or show it. We are not nerds. They eat at another table. They do dumb things like have farting contests, which I don't like while I'm eating.

At our table we make cool jokes that sometimes make fun of others, like the super jocks who spend their time flexing their muscles and talking constantly about sports and stuff like that. We don't mean to be bullies, and we aren't. We just keep our thoughts at our table. We make jokes about each other, too, and we laugh a lot, sometimes to the point of not being cool.

Then there are the food fights—at least that's what we call them. Grownups think food fights are silly, kind of immature. They are probably right, but then they don't get the skill of food fighting. It's not the amount of food you send across the room. It's the skill with which you throw it. We all like the little green peas that are served with mashed potatoes. The peas aren't that good. Besides, they are green. The good thing is how small they are and how nicely they work in a spoon. The spoon can fling them just right so the person you want to get it is hit dead center. There is a science to a well-run food fight, but Sidney will never understand it. This leads to the second skill. That is sending the little green missile when Sidney or one of the lunch-room supervisors is not looking.

Sometimes we get into a burping contest. I will admit it is probably something we should have gotten out of our systems during elementary school, but there is something about gulping air and then burping it up as long as you can, kind of like an opera singer trying to hold onto a note. The whole point is to gross people out. The sounds made by your body as it gets rid of the pressure are not like anything else you will ever hear.

Then there's the sound made by other kinds of pressure, if you get what I mean. Farting is like an art. Some kids do a lot of it in the lunch room. Jeff says the seventh-graders don't find it as funny as we do. At the lunch table, when we cut one, everybody breaks up. Maybe we are more like the apes and chimpanzees than we think. Some people are really good with the "silent but deadly" ones. They give it away, though, by sort of tipping to one side. Others make the noise of a big bass vibration and all that. It is the same thing as a musical solo but with the other end.

I hope all this hasn't ruined your appetite.

BEING COOL

In middle school, maybe the most important thing is to be cool. There are some kids who think they are cool, but they are not. The guys who think they are cool kind of walk different, sort of like they have Jell-O for butts. They walk slow, with a kind of "notice me" thing. They ooze down the hall, floating above the rest of us. Their shoes sort of bounce off the floor and it looks like they have ball bearings in their knees. Guys like that get laughed at a lot.

Then there are the really cool dudes. They wear their style like a loose coat, never seeming to notice others like them. There is something at work here. When you think you are cool, you probably are not. When you don't even think about being cool, you probably are. Another way of saying it is: when you try, you fail; when you don't, you succeed.

I don't think I am popular, but I don't know. My mom says not to care, so I have tried to ignore the whole thing. Inside I know I am cool enough. Being popular costs a lot, and I don't think I want to pay the price. My mom says to just be me. I hope she's right. Parents always try to make you feel good.

There are other signs of being cool. One is how you dress. Clothes are important. I didn't think they were until recently. My mom used to buy my clothes, and what she picked didn't bother me. Now it does. She bought me a shirt with flowers on it, for cripes' sake. I said to her, "Mom, I can't wear that. They'll think I'm gay." Mom said she thought the shirt was sweet. I told her that was the whole point.

I like clothes with brand names on them and sweats and things like that. Sports team shirts are OK, but you have to be careful that people don't think you are just a jock who has played too much football without your helmet on.

Personally, I don't like the saggy pants. Some kids look cool when they wear them, but you could always be panted. No reason to tempt. In case you don't know what that means, it is when someone pulls your pants down in front of everyone. Some people think it is hilarious; I think it is gross. I wear a belt, just to be safe.

To be cool, you also have to give off a kind of manly odor. That means you need to let your sweats kind of mature, if you get what I mean. Then you need a splash on some aftershave, even if you have never used a razor. The kind of aftershave is really, really important. You don't want to smell too flowery. Some guys walk by and you could just die from the odor. They smell like a bouquet, not manly at all. It's better to smell more like a cross between a cedar closet and dried leaves.

The way you speak is also important. You have to know a kind of language. Maybe you could call it "cool-ese." It means you say just enough, not too much. Motor-mouthing is definitely not cool. Words like "yep" and "nope" are definitely in. "Man" and "dude" go in certain circles. In fact, the word "cool" itself is important, used a lot. Then there is "wicked," which can mean "wow" or "cool" or even "bad." Your facial expressions and how you use the words make you cool. I am just learning some of the cool language, but I'm getting better.

Oh yeah, while I'm at it, let me tell you about "gay." The word isn't what it used to be. It certainly doesn't mean "happy." Sometimes it means a weird thing: "That's gay, man." "What a gay thing to do." Or it can be a way of bullying someone: "You're gay." Most of the time it has nothing to do with actually being gay—liking someone of your own sex, if you know what I mean. It just means not the usual thing and all that. It's weird, but you can be gay and cool. But a lot of the guys use the word "gay" to mean the opposite of "cool."

There are definitely some seriously uncool things you'd better not do. The most serious thing is never to kiss or be kissed by your mother in front of the guys. This is very uncool. A simple "bye, Mom" won't get you in trouble, but allowing motherly affection is a no-no. I have seriously warned my mom. So far she has paid attention.

It is very uncool to overdo a laugh, especially a nerdy one. A nerdy laugh is like a honk, sort of gooselike, what you hear in fall migrations. A cool laugh is kind of like a suppressed burp, a snicker with your lip and nose slightly turned up. Laughing cool is kind of a skill.

It is uncool to tell your guy friends how much you like them. You can tell them they are cool. They will appreciate that. You can also hit them on the shoulder, but never on the butt, unless you're on the football team. "You're

OK, dude" is alright, but that's about as far as you should go. In middle school, "I love you, man" is definitely out.

It is uncool to show off openly. This is true in school subjects and in sports too. The rule is simple: let people see how good you are for themselves. If you are smart in school, people will find out. If you are a whiz in sports, it will show. When people tell you how good you are, don't overdo the "aw, shucks" stuff. Just say, with your eyes down a little, "thanks."

There are many other uncool things we all do. There are several in these chronicles. A very uncool thing to do is be too ready to answer a question in class. Only nerds and geeks wave their hands around; sometimes, God forbid, they even say, "Oh, me, me, let me answer that." This is really, really uncool. If you know the answer and are cool, you kind of slouch in your seat and sort of lightly wave your hand with your elbow on the desk. Your message is "It doesn't matter to me, but I will give you the answer if you really want it."

Texting is definitely in. Cool texting is really something to admire. That means texting during class without the teacher figuring it out. Sometimes it's fun to text across the room, or "rm" in text-speak. If the teacher ever sees you or reads what you've texted, you are still cool but now also in trouble. "OMG I ht la soooo boring. Zzzzz" would probably get Fobbs into a major clutch-up. LOL.

I guess the height of coolness is being slick in talking to girls. I am not good at it yet. My face turns red, and the words don't come out right. It's really weird, since a girl is only a junior version of your mom. Guys that are majorly cool know how to kind of slither over to the girls' table and start a conversation. Dude talk from the street is out. "Hey, baby" will get you sent away from the table. Just a "hey" or "how are ya" will do. Cool guys don't ever look stressed or worked up when they talk to a girl. I am afraid I don't know how to do that yet.

There is a cool way of standing. You kind of let one hip be lower than the other. One foot is nearly at a right angle to the other. Then you sort of shift your weight back and forth as if you were bored or waiting or just passing time. It is kind of hard to explain, but when you see it, there is no doubt it is cool.

I am still studying being cool. Honestly, though, I am not sure if it is worth it.

FIGHTS

A fight was on yesterday. One kid, Ralph, called another kid, Tim, a wimp and a wuss and all that. He even used some really bad words to insult Tim. Tim is a quiet kid, but he weighs more than most of us, and he is stronger than you would think. Ralph is an athlete, or thinks he is, and he uses this language to make a point, although I don't know exactly what that is.

Tim had enough and finally told Ralph he was going to beat the you-know-what out of him. Ralph's mouth wouldn't stop, so eventually the fight was on in the back hall down by the gym. Teachers don't go there much unless they are sneaking out for a smoke in their cars.

A crowd gathered because we all knew what was going on. The fight began as usual, with pushing back and forth, some threats, and some seriously nasty looks. Finally Ralph threw a punch. He never expected what happened next. Tim hit him several times and made his nose bleed. He would probably still be hitting Ralph if we hadn't pulled him off.

Then Ralph did a really embarrassing thing. He started to cry. Tim tried to explain that he hadn't meant to hurt him but that Ralph had to stop calling him a wuss and a wimp and all the other names too.

Ralph said he wouldn't do it again, ever. They shook hands. Ralph has a lot to live down. Crying in front of the dudes is not cool, but he had it coming. I guess the story has many morals, if you know what I mean. The first is don't mess with Tim unless you have the muscle to back it up. The second is to use your mouth for better things. The third is do not cry in front of the dudes. Then, again, maybe it just proves how useless fighting is in the first place.

Most fights never happen. They are all talk, with push-ing and shoving. Most people really don't like to fight, but they think if they back down, they will be called names. I wonder what takes more manhood, if you know what I mean: beating someone up, or taking it and walking away. I haven't had to choose yet, but it's probably coming.

I don't like to fight, but I will if I have to. It looks like that is the way it's going to go with Bob Jersey. He has been in my classes for the past few years, and I have tried to ignore him. He is kind of a bully, not by being mean but by perfecting being obnoxious. The problem is he's had a "growth spurt," as the grownups like to call it. It just means he is bigger than he used to be so his obnoxious-ness is more gross and disgusting. Aside from the fact that he smells, he has taken to doing annoying things. When you think about it, the name Jersey is right close to "jerk."

Last year in elementary school, Jersey thought it was fun to lift his shirt and put his hand under his armpits. When he moved his arm up and down, it made a kind of farting sound. To top it off, he liked to chase the girls with the hand that had been under his arm. The smell was not too sweet.

Jersey "panted" one kid in gym. This is not new around here, but Jersey thought it was the funniest thing he had ever done. It is embarrassing when your underwear is out there for everyone to see, if you know what I mean. The kid he panted is kind of shy and wound up getting real upset, for which he was sent to guidance to see Mr. Strong, who, by the way, wears his pants halfway up his chest.

Well, Jersey decided he would try one of his stunts with me. He gave me a "wet willy." Let me try to explain just how disgusting a wet willy is and why from Jersey it was even grosser than a regular willy, if there is such a thing.

A wet willy means sucking on one of your fingers and getting it wet with spit. Then you go up to someone and stick your wet finger in their ear. When you aren't looking for it, a wet one can be a shock. And when other people see it happen, it can make you really angry.

Jersey came from behind in the hall and willied me. His nasty finger is dirty enough, but it was covered with his disgusting spit that he put in my ear. His one friend, a real goofball, practically fell on the floor laughing.

I have told Jersey what I think of his pranks and that I will beat the wetness right out of him. He kind of swelled up and said, "Come on, Kevin, go ahead and do it." I told him to watch out, so things are on hold right now.

Personally, I hope things stay on hold. Outside I can talk tough, but inside I don't like to fight. Melissa agrees with me and has been in my corner about the whole thing. Fighting is really stupid. You would think with evolution and all that, human beings would have gotten over it.

On the other hand, if Jersey keeps up his bullying, I will do my very best to make him remember not to mess with me. If he wins the fight, I have promised myself I will not cry.

If you get into a fight, it can be tough. You will go see Sidney, who will go on and on about why this never happens at Birch Meadow, even though it does. You will do time with Mr. Strong, who will want to see you and the other kid so you can "work things out between the two of you." Imagine having to sit in Strong's office with Jersey and make nice and all that, even when I would rather be punching the kid in the nose. I am going to try not to fight Jersey, but it may not be something I can avoid.

It wasn't really a fight but just horsing around that got me two detentions earlier in the year. A friend of mine and I were just having a good time. We were sort of hitting each other with our gloves, fooling around. Ms. Fobbs, the LA fiend, came down the hall and acted like a cop. We tried to explain that we were just kidding, but she said she knew a fight when she saw one and wrote us up for it. She said she would escort us to the office. LA teachers don't walk. They escort. Neither Ms. Fobbs or Sidney seemed interested in hearing our side of the story. We both had to go for detentions, which just made the school day longer. At least this time Sidney didn't send us to Mr. Strong, thank God.

Name calling is annoying. My dad says it goes along with the age of kids in my grade and through the middle-school years. He says the kids who do it will get tired of it eventually. When we were younger, it was names like "jerk" or even "retard." Now it is "homo," "gay," "queer," or others like that. Dad says the reason boys call others by these names is they are afraid they are what the names mean. So if I call you a name, that makes you the guy who is like that name, not me. Maybe Dad's right, but the names can get old and make you really mad inside.

THINGS YOU WON'T BELIEVE

Now you have the idea of middle school. This is only part of the story. The next few stories are all true, but sometimes they are kind of mature, if you know what I mean. Some parents might be upset or think this kind of thing never happens in any school. We can all be sorry for parents who don't know much about people our age, but it is probably a good idea to have them read this section so they can at least understand it.

THE SCHOOL BUS

My school bus picks me up every morning about seven o'clock. Then it brings me home in the afternoon when school lets out. A guy named Malcolm drives the bus. His name about says it all. He looks kind of bored, but who wouldn't be driving a school bus? I don't think Malcolm likes his job. I don't think he likes us much, either. When I get on in the morning I always say, "Hi, Malcolm." He says, "Hmpph" or something close to that. The only time Malcolm ever speaks is when he is really pissed. Then he rolls his words together sort of loud. "Al rightyouguysenoughofthatsitdownanddon'tletmehearfro myouagain." Then he takes a breath and sometimes says, "Didgahearme?" Malcolm is never really happy with us except around holidays, when he kind of smiles. I think it is because he knows he won't have to drive the bus for a few days and won't be seeing us.

All of us on the bus go to middle school. When I first went to sixth grade in the fall, I learned what to do when you get on the bus. The eighth-graders get first pick. I sat in a seat I liked. Then two stops later this eighth-grader got on. He came to my seat and looked at me. He said, "Move." He was a lot bigger than I am. I wanted to say, "Hey, dude, do you see your name on this seat?," but I didn't. I moved. I was afraid he would think I was a pussy, but it turned out we became sort of friends. He looks out for me if someone else in his grade gives me a hard time. I think he is kind of like the lion in the story where the boy took a thorn out of the lion's foot, and the boy and lion became friends.

You can think of the school bus as a yellow classroom on wheels. Malcolm is definitely not a teacher, but the kids instruct each other in all sorts of things. There's a lot of teasing. Sometimes it becomes angry and more like bullying. There is swearing. Take, for instance, the f-word. It is definitely big, and I don't remember learning much swearing in the fifth grade. The eighth-graders swear a lot and with a kind of skill. It's like a greeting: "Hey, eff you." Then a friend says, "Eff you, too." It's actually kind of friendly, and no one really means it, if you know what I mean. The f-word just sounds wicked, like you are a real man and grown up and smell of sweat and aftershave.

Some of the swearing is pretty advanced. When I say advanced, I mean the swearing is more descriptive. For example, everyone can use the f-word, but some guys get really creative with it. They can use it as an adjective, a noun, or a verb. Man, the f-word is useful, when you think about it. So you might think of swearing on the bus as a kind of practical application of language arts. It would be fun to write an essay about skill in using the f-word, but that would probably land you in guidance, maybe even a session with Sidney.

No one swears in front of the teachers although once one of the teachers lost it with his class and told them they were a bunch of "little spoiled bastards." I guess I can say "bastards" since it only means having sort of mixed-up parentage. The teacher got in trouble for perverting young minds. One of the parents was furious and called Sidney, who probably agreed with the teacher but wanted to make things look good and keep his job.

I wonder who invented swearing? Maybe the cavemen did when they hit their hands with a rock, or did they say the same things your dad does when he messes up hanging Mom's new curtains? But swearing has proba-bly improved and grown with the times. Mom says you could not say "suck" when she was a kid because it meant something else. Dad said the word "piss" would get your mouth washed out with soap. That's when he was young. I don't know what you are supposed to say, but "piss" just sounds like what it is, like the poems Mrs. Fobbs tells us about that have the sounds of what they are talking about in them. I have not read a poem with the word "piss" in it, at least not yet.

Swears have a lot to do with sex, although I don't quite get it. The f-word really is more about being manly, even angry and all that. I didn't know it had anything to do with sex until the fourth grade. I only knew my parents got pale when I came home and asked, "What does 'f---' mean?" Dad said, "Your mother will tell you" and went to watch a football game. Then Mom started with, "Well, Kevin, there is male and female." God, I hate that opening. Her explanation was kind of technical, but I got the idea.

The jokes and talk about sex really wake you up to what's going on. Think about it. The bees are messing around. Even the plants in the garden are cross-pollinating. There's all this sex going on all around you. The school bus just brings the whole thing home. It makes you think about all the things people do as sex.

My pastor says we are all made in the image of God. If that's true, God must die laughing and have a great sense of humor. In fact, maybe God rode the school bus when he was in middle school, but they probably never had them back then.

One of the things we do like to do on the bus is make jokes about people's names. Some parents should think about the bus when they are naming their kids. Others can't help it because their last names just lend themselves to ridicule.

Some kids have a lot of trouble with their names. Maybe it is kind of like art, but we all love to make names sound different—not nicknames but sort of making fun. It really isn't like bullying, but it can get nasty, if you know what I mean. Some kids just have names other people love to mock.

There's this nice kid in school, kind of quiet, but with a name everyone makes fun of. Not of him, just his name.

His last name is Pomfert. You have to admit, that is kind of a queer name and all, but some kids started calling him "Porn Fart" or "Porn Foot" and stuff like that. At first I laughed, but I could tell he was about to cry. It kind of makes you feel helpless because there's not much you can do about your name. Since then Pomfert and I have become friends. I call him by his first name, Ben. That keeps me from slipping and saying Porn Fart by accident.

In grade school the school bus was noisy but tame. Now the bus reminds me I am growing up.

FRED

Maybe one of the weirdest things I did this year is about my friend Fred. How it all came about was my mom's fault. She wasn't thinking and she made a salami sandwich for lunch, which she knows I don't like at all. The sandwich was on a kind of bun. I put the sandwich in my locker. I knew it was salami, and I never planned to eat it. On that day I bummed some lunch from my friend Jeff.

Let me tell you about lockers in the middle school. In elementary school we didn't have lockers, at least not at the one I attended. I thought it was great in middle school to have a new place, a kind of home where you could put all your stuff. Within about a week of the start of school, my locker was stacked with stuff. It was what my mom calls a "pig sty." This has never made sense to me since I always thought a sty was something you got in your eye, and I could never figure out what it has to do with pigs.

Anyway, my salami sandwich got buried in my locker, and I forgot about it until I discovered it in mid-November. By that time it had grown whiskers and turned kind of green. It had a smell you wouldn't forget. I was about to throw it away when it dawned on me something special could happen with my sandwich. It could be a pet, a kind of school mascot. Think about it. No one at Hogwarts ever had a sandwich for a pet. Why not?

So I named my sandwich Fred, Fred the pet sandwich. You would never let a pet run around without a leash, so I made one out of yarn in art class. The leash was sort of multi-colored and neat. Fred liked his new leash, and I did too.

It was only a matter of time before Fred became known to the other kids. No teacher ever heard about Fred, of course, and Sidney sure didn't know about him. He would have freaked out and probably given detentions for having a pet sandwich. Imagine being written up. Offense: "Student has a pet sandwich." But my classmates knew him. And as Fred became better known, even popular, kids asked if he could visit their lockers. Fred got around and became a school legend. By Christmas he had turned completely black and hard. His leash blended with his new color. He seemed to like going from locker to locker, and one of my friends asked if he could have Fred over the holidays. There was a code around Fred. No parent or teacher was ever to be told about his existence.

Fred went home to many houses on weekends, but no one ever revealed his place at Birch Meadow. Fred was quiet. He never caused anybody any trouble. His body odor disappeared with time, and he became more socially acceptable. My friends Jeff and Carl kind of coparented him.

Now that the year is coming to an end, Fred will go home with me for the summer. Fred is getting more brittle with age, and some kind of decent burial will probably happen when school is out and the weather gets warm. Fred is getting tired. All the attention and moving around from locker to locker has been a strain on him.

When you think about it, the life span of a sandwich is probably only about a year, even for a remarkable salami sandwich like Fred.

I have never liked salami, but I will really miss Fred. My friends will miss him too. I think I will keep his leash as a reminder of the special sandwich who really got around at Birch Meadow.

My locker is still a mess. Fred and I like it that way.

THE BATTLE OF THE BANDS

Jeff saw me on the way to the john. "Hey, dude, you won't believe what I can tell you when I see you at noon." Even though Jeff has a different lunch hour, we can catch some time together between classes.

Lunch could not come fast enough for me that day, but it wasn't because I was hungry. It was because Jeff usually didn't get this excited unless there was something really great to tell me.

There was.

"Dude," Jeff began, "have you ever heard of The Purple Helmet?" I hadn't, so he explained. Jeff said there was a big fuss going on about the name "Purple Helmet."

It turns out it was, and I guess is, a rock group in our school.

The thing about this group is not their music. It all started when Sidney, bless his wizard-like heart, decided there should be a battle of the bands.

This was big news in Birch Meadow, and Sidney was especially proud of bringing our humble middle school into the musical mainstream. Sure enough, there was more than a little excitement about the whole thing.

Mr. Dawn, the music teacher, was as excited as Sidney. Two Fridays ago the battle had taken place. I didn't go, since bands in middle school are usually mostly loud drumming and amps blaring with no one who knows how to play.

As Jeff talked, I remembered hearing that the winner had been a group called The Purple Helmet. I didn't think much about it but had heard nothing else about the band or their performance. The battle was over so far as I was concerned.

Jeff said the trouble began when Sidney discovered the meaning of the name for the band.

I was puzzled, so Jeff tried to give me a clue. "Hey, man, it's about your stuff." I didn't know what he meant at first. I thought he was talking about my locker or my backpack. "You know," Jeff continued, "your thing." My mind wasn't in the same place as Jeff's, so he got more specific. He pointed at my crotch.

"Oh," I said. It dawned on me what Jeff was talking about.

"Think about it," he said. "The tip of your thing looks like..."

"A purple helmet," I said.

The band is a group of Goth-type kids who think they are already in the big time. Some people say they smoke pot, and it is rumored girls have seen their purple helmets, if you know what I mean. They don't have tattoos yet, or piercings, either, but they do have those belts with metal things on them. The guys are in the eighth grade, so I don't know them.

It turned out Sidney had asked one of the band members where they got their name. He probably thought it was from mythology or something like that and wanted to advance education. The band member told him. Sidney got a quick advance to his education. He almost stroked out and has been in overdrive ever since.

He has used words like "vile" and "depraved," whatever that means.

The meaning went all over school, except I never heard about it. Parents were alarmed. Sidney was nonstop on the phone. Mr. Dawn, the music teacher, took some days off to recover.

Sidney was really burned about his introduction of the group on the evening of the battle of the bands. As I heard it, Sidney introduced the group by saying, "I want to introduce a great, standup group of guys who really know how to do it: The Purple Helmet." The few who knew the meaning of the name broke up in laughter.

Later, when Sidney understood what he had done, he was not amused. He came on the P.A. with kind of gag order. He said a "vile" thing had happened at our dear school that would forever stain our reputation. He said we could not mention this to anyone. The whole thing was to be buried...forever! Of course, that meant we all started talking about nothing else.

The kids have had a great time with the whole battle thing. We asked Mrs. Fobbs what "depraved" meant. She said she did not wish to discuss it.

That's why there is a whole lot of excitement in the principal's office. Even Miss Emma is tight lipped. She wants to know nothing about purple helmets.

God, being in middle school is educational.

THE EIGHTH-GRADE CLASS TRIP

The eighth grade takes a trip to Washington, DC every year. They are back now, and people are talking about stuff from their trip. They like telling what they did, at least the guys I have heard about do. One class tells what was better about their trip than the previous eighth grade and so on. It's kind of fun for us to hear we have to look forward to.

You're probably thinking the stories are about how our government works, the Lincoln places, and stuff like that. They do talk about those things, but the main details are about what went on in the hotel in Virginia. That's where they stayed.

Before the trip there is a parents' meeting. They are told about how well supervised the trip is and how strict the rules are and all that. Sidney is at his best as he talks about the no-nonsense rules. You know. The zero-tolerance thing. This puts the parents' minds at ease.

For the kids, it is a challenge to see what things they can do without being caught. One of the things the chaperones do is to place some tape on each door when it is time for bed. This is so no one can get out or in until it is morning and time for breakfast. Thirteen- and fourteen-year-old brains like to meet the challenge. How do you get the tape off your door, put it back, and escape the eyes of your faithful chaperone, usually a teacher? The guys have told me it isn't as hard as it sounds. I hope we can learn to do the same thing when we go to DC.

Anyway, the trip leaves early in the morning, and the class arrives at the hotel late in the evening. They stay in DC for four nights. The four guys we heard about spent their evening learning if their trick to remove and replace the tape worked. It did. So the next night they went for a shopping trip. Each room had a window. They were on the fifth floor, and the idea of making water bombs was on their minds. They needed something rubber. On the shopping trip, the idea of buying some condoms sounded really neat. They felt kind of full of sin, they said, even though they planned to just load the condoms with water and drop them out of the hotel window. Condoms are perfect for water bombs. Everyone knows condoms can stand a lot and shouldn't leak. The guys were really careful about being sure the tape was in place and they also were very neat, not leaving any traces of water on the window sill. Apparently one of their bombs splashed on the pavement in front of a hotel guest, who got really pissed. The chaperones checked the tape, which was in place, and told the hotel manager it couldn't be one of their kids. When the manager and one of the teachers came up to check, the guys were in bed, reading some books. There was no water on the sill or anywhere else. The condoms were hidden. There was no evidence to convict. No jury would ever believe they were the Best Western water bombers, these nice kids from Birch Meadow.

That was the second night. During the day the guys had been reading the movie list in a folder in the room. There were some real terrific-sounding titles in the "adults only" section. *"Amazing Sluts* and *I Was a Crazed Teen Lover* were a couple of ones I remember from what the guys said. The teachers had told the kids the channel for the porn movies was blocked. It was. So the guys plotted how to get it back on. The idea was to call when the night clerk was on and speak with a deep voice. One of the guys in the room has grown faster, and he has a voice like a man. His voice can pass for adult when he really works at it. He called the desk and said the channel could be restored in that room. The kids would be somewhere else. Sure enough, the guy turned on the channel. The guys will not say what happened after that. I'm not sure I want to know.

The best thing was the last thing they did. It was their last night. They were really hungry, so they ordered three pizzas to share. They only ate two, leaving one entire pizza. Since they couldn't take it to another room, they needed to do something with it in their room.

They decided it would be great to stick the pizza on the ceiling of the room. One of the guys is really tall, and he stood on the bed and pushed the pizza onto the ceiling. It stuck in place.

The next day, the boys left for home. The pizza, still stuck to the ceiling, stayed. Now, the thing we all see as funny is what we imagined happening next. The maids would come clean the room, but they'd never look at the ceiling. They would dust and sweep with their vacuums, trying to move on to the next room. Then the room would get used by the next person. When they lie down in bed, they'd look up and see a pizza on the ceiling. They'd call the manager and tell him, "Hey, there's a pizza on the ceiling of my room." Imagine the manager: "I wonder what that guy has been drinking. He's seeing pizzas on the ceiling." No one would ever figure it was the eighth-grade guys from Birch Meadow.

I hope our class can come up with some good stuff to do when we take the eighth-grade trip.

THE SCHOOL DANCE

I could hardly wait for the first school dance, which was in the fall. But let me tell you, it wasn't like what I thought it would be. I had heard a lot about the dances at middle school. The sixth grade has its own dances. There are four in the whole school year. I have been to three and am kind of an expert now. Maybe the seventh-grade dances will be different, but I will tell you about ours.

The best thing about our dances is not the girls. It's the food. There's pizza, Coke, sandwiches, and chips. You can keep coming through the line until you get all you want.

The girls get mad because the guys don't dance with them, at least until they come and get us. When we see one coming, we head into the boys' locker room off the gym. Girls can't come in there. To be honest, girls are no competition for pizza.

The music is loud. Most of the time we can't understand the words that are being sung, but the beat is good and kind of exciting. The dances are usually hip-hop or rock, but every so often there is a slow one.

None of us want the girls to figure out we can't dance. My dad said all I had to do was bounce up and down and make motions with my hands. He said to pretend I was doing things like shoveling snow, swatting flies, or buttering toast. With the hand movements and the bouncing, I am not bad. When there is a slow dance, that's the best time to go to the boys' room. If a girl asks you to dance slow, then the best thing to do is rock back and forth with your hands around her neck.

The eighth grade had their dances called off because they were doing some stuff that honest to God doesn't sound that fun. They call it "grinding." My dad said it's like lap dancing standing up. It turns out the eighth-graders were getting excited by the whole thing, so Sidney canceled the dances until the kids got control of themselves.

One time I was asked by this girl if I wanted to dance. She was a foot taller than I am and sort of developed, if you know what I mean. It turned out to be a slow dance, so I let her decide how we would go about it. My face was about where she was sort of present. It was embarrassing, and the guys all teased me about it. They said they wondered if I could breathe and all that.

As I said, the music is loud, and the gym or "cafetorium" is decorated. Our gym is what they call "multi-purpose." Even with decorations you know where you are because you can still smell the gym socks.

At one of the seventh-grade dances, something happened that almost got theirs canceled just like the eighth grade. At some dances there is kind of a break. Parents, who are there as chaperones, bring out punch on a rolling table.

The punch is usually the kind made with sherbet and ginger ale. It is green glop, but it tastes good, and the parents are members of the PTA, so we all act like we like it.

The dance was set for around Christmas time. The table came out with a holiday cloth on it and special cups. One of the chaperones, the lady who was president of the PTA, took the punch bowl ladle and scooped the first drink. Only there wasn't just punch. The ladle came up with a jock strap on it. I guess I should call it an athletic supporter, but that always sounds like someone who attends all the pep rallies.

I guess you could say the crowd gasped, especially the adults. The kids tried to keep a straight face, but laughter got the best of everyone. Kids made a lot of jokes like "Dude, that's what I call spiking the punch."

The table was rolled back into the kitchen. No holiday punch was served. The PTA president had to go home. Sidney was in a fine fit.

He said he would get to the bottom of it since, in his memory, no one had ever put a jock strap in the punch before. He used words like "depraved" again. My dad said that meant it was pretty bad, but he was smiling when he said it.

Our sixth-grade dances have not been this much fun, and they don't serve holiday punch anymore.

Sidney's investigation is ongoing, but no one knows who did it. They say Sidney has tried to identify the jock strap but has had no luck. I'll bet whoever did it is glad his mom didn't put his name on it.

The final dance is coming up. It is supposed to be a kind of formal. You don't have to wear a tie, but a white shirt is required. I don't know what the thing is about white shirts. Some of the guys are asking girls out for this one.

I may ask someone out by myself. I don't know if I will ask Six Cents or Twilla Light or no one. Lots of guys go by themselves. Melissa and I are friends, and she might go with me. The problem is the dork she is going out with now will probably take her. Life with girls and dances and social stuff can get very complicated.

ONE LAST CHAPTER DEDICATED TO MRS. FOBBS

THE ASSIGNMENT: WHAT I HAVE LEARNED

Mrs. Fobbs asked the class to write a few things about what we have learned this year in middle school. I listed serious and funny things I have learned. Sometimes it was hard to tell them apart. Mrs. Fobbs gave me a C on my assignment. I think she missed the whole reason I wrote what I wrote. She is not famous for having a great sense of humor. Most English teachers aren't. I will list some of my thoughts and let you be the judge.

Not-Serious Things:

Farting is a real art.

You should avoid adults who eat gross cucumber-and-sour-cream stuff for lunch.

Some teachers are actually hot, but not too many.

Girls are complicated, but you probably already know that.

School nurses with bottles and spoons are dangerous.

School buses are where you learn stuff you will never hear in school.

Some teachers haven't paid attention and still sneak out for a smoke.

Sydney is a dork, but he is our dork!

Frazier is cool.

Jock straps in the punch bowl can wreck a school dance.

Miss Emma is a doll but a kind of big one.

You'd better know what something means before you make introductions at band battles.

Most things that are "symbols" in language arts are stupid.

Some eighth-graders like to grind.

Wet willies are disgusting.

Always wear a belt unless you like being "panted."

Serious Things:

Barf on a bun actually tastes good when you have it with friends. The friends make up for the bad cooking.

Being cool is probably not worth the effort.

Fighting doesn't solve anything.

You can't hurry growing up.

Smart people do some really dumb things.

Getting older doesn't necessarily mean getting smarter.

Most teachers really care.

Never drink the punch at school dances.

Unless you know what a word means, it is best not to use it.

Skipping school can floor you.

A leftover sandwich is a leftover sandwich.

Strong chairs can prevent embarrassment.

Middle school is where you learn important things about people, and that includes yourself.

Uncool friends are still friends, sometimes the best ones you have.

Important people are often not really that important.

Unimportant people make things happen.

Swearing just makes you sound ridiculous.

Becoming a man takes time. It's probably true for girls and women too.

WHO IS KEVIN?

Kevin is the voice of Dr. Larry Larsen, a clinical psychologist in Andover, Massachusetts. Dr. Larsen has worked with children, adolescents, and their families for over forty years. According to Dr. Larsen "Kevin is really the voice of countless middle school students I have known. In that sense he actually wrote the book and is speaking for them." Dr. Larsen brings humor to the book based on real experiences. "They are actual stories which kids have told me, but they are fictionalized," he said.

The sketches in the book were drawn by David Ammons, an amateur artist, who read the book and captured the personalities of people Kevin described.

Made in the USA
Charleston, SC
10 June 2014